Surf The Waves

(Czarina Book 1)

OrangeBooks Publication

Smriti Nagar, Bhilai, Chhattisgarh - 490020

Website: **www.orangebooks.in**

© **Copyright, 2020, Author**

All rights reserved. No part of this book may be reproduced, stored in a retrieval system, or transmitted, in any form by any means, electronic, mechanical, magnetic, optical, chemical, manual, photocopying, recording or otherwise, without the prior written consent of its writer.

First Edition, 2020

ISBN: 978-93-90169-40-5

Price: Rs.120.00

The opinions/ contents expressed in this book are solely of the author and do not represent the opinions/ standings/ thoughts of OrangeBooks.

Printed in India

101 TIPS TO BECOME THE BEST WORKING MOM

Surf The Waves

Water | Air | Vulcan (Fire) | Earth | Space

NEHAL. VRK
EDITED BY: RANDIE CREAMER

OrangeBooks Publication
www.orangebooks.in

Dedicated to My Mom, Kunjbala Patel

Describing my mother would be to write about a hurricane in its perfect power, or the rising and falling of colors of a rainbow.

Every life has its challenges, so did my mother's too. But she showered all that she had on us, and remain empty. She Filled Our Lives with Richness of Thoughts and Warmth of ♥Love. No thanks can be sufficed.....for that creation of God who is called - Mommy. Love ♥ You Mom.

Xpertink Writing Services

Freelance Writing Services

Email – neha.writereditor@gmail.com

Website- https://authornehalvrk.com
https://xpertink.co.in/our-blogs/

Facebook-https://www.facebook.com/nehalsbook/
https://www.facebook.com/nehalvishal.agrawal
Instagram-https://www.instagram.com/author_nehal.vrk/

Acknowledgments

This book would not possible without the support of my daughter Annie and my better half, Vishal Agrawal. I am thankful to Vishal for always being there, understanding my work, and taking care of all my needs in my day-to-day life.

And my princess, Annie, for always being there when I need to discuss some point while writing and giving me insightful suggestions and solutions. With her support, I was able to create what I'd envisioned. Each day she stuns me more. I am thankful to God who has gifted me with a lovely family.

My writing career is due to the vision of my father and mother, who support me for my career in any case. And guide me what should I do. I pray to God may I get these parents in every life. And I am also thankful for having my son Raunak, whose love is my strength. Without his presence I may fail to think and deliver the things the way I do.

To all my family, your support is endless and everlasting.

Thanks for making my dream come true.

Hey You, Working Mom!

My first and foremost word to you is:

"God has created you as an artist.

You just have to master the Art of Motherhood!"

Your life may seem difficult, but a little juggling will make you

Happy... Happier... and Happiest!

Here is an ode to you and your zeal:

Don't let your struggle diminish your persona.

Instead, flourish your divinity. O, Mommy!

———

Index

Introduction	1
We All Are One Tribe!	2
The Waves Inside You	4
The Water	10
The Air	14
The Vulcan	25
The Earth	33
The Space	39
Quick Tips	42
The Spouse Help	44
The Five Unique Qualities	49
How to Use This Guide	51

Introduction

Being a mom is special, and being a working mom? It's simply – super special.

My goal in writing this book is to help you release the guilt that whispers in your ears, "Being a working mom is going to take a toll on your children." Believe me, it will not. Perhaps you have not realized, but your profession is an asset to your life, and it will eventually benefit your children and family in a multitude of ways. All that you need right now is the warm assurance that being a working mommy will not lead you on a guilt trip; instead, it will help you travel the road of self-improvement.

Fall in love with your dual roles of being a mother and a professional. It is incredible how kids change your life, especially your professional life. Without them, working would be boring and feel like nothing but long, dry hours. However, having the financial security from working allows for a more enriching family, even when juggling both careers.

This book has been crafted uniquely for young working mothers, for them take pride in themselves for all they are capable of. It is loaded with practical advice by experienced working mothers, and hopefully it will help you strike that "golden balance."

Trust Me - You Can, and You Will.

We All Are One Tribe!

If you are juggling homework, social engagements, tutoring, maintaining your family's health, travel, holidays, weekend planning, grocery shopping, laundering, cooking, house repair, etc., you are an eligible member of the "Working Mom's Tribe."

In every town across the world, there are women like you who are the emotional glue for their family. It is time to take pride in yourself and stand with your head held high.

Here is a list of prominent roles that a working mom like you has probably experienced:

- You are the quiz master who has an answer to all the whos, hows, whys, whens and whats thrown at her.

- You care enough to think about every need of your family and make everyone feel appreciated.

- You are equally responsible for your own career and professional obligations without any concessions.

- You are round-the-clock, torturing yourself doing unseen, unheard, and unappreciated jobs of daily life.

- You are taken for granted for whatever you have done, are doing, and will be doing.

The changes within the 21st century are helping to change the way we think and behave, which nourishes our tribe. We are multiplying each day. Even in countries that firmly follow a patriarchal pattern, women are now working and excelling in their careers. Women are proving that we are not only good enough to be in the kitchen, but we are reaching the new peaks and spreading success all over the planet!

So, I congratulate you for being a part of this tribe, and I wish you all luck in balancing motherhood and a career. Just remember, you can do it. Follow the tips given in the book, and you will find everything you need to sort your time out!

The Waves Inside You

Women and Five Elements

*O, Woman, you are a creator
and a nurturer – like Mother Nature.*

A woman has waves inside her. Believe me. You have all five, because... God has gifted you.

Women—precisely like mighty nature—can maintain those five elements that make her all mighty! The waves consist of: water, air, vulcan (fire), earth, and space. The building blocks of all the materialistic existence are akin to the qualities of a woman's persona. You must be thinking: How? Let me explain...

Water

Water is calm and flowing. A perfect metaphor for a woman who is gentle and unruffled, yet who can transform herself into a solid state during trying times. Both are similar as they connect, protect, and nourish. Women nourish their families, but at the same time there is the opportunity for pain and a flood of emotions if they get hurt by the family they are caring for.

Water is the element of passion and wisdom—exactly like women. Women are born with emotional intelligence, allowing us to cherish the relationships and mental health of our families.

Air

Air, like women, is light, ever-moving, and ready to change, always on the go and adaptable to varied situations. It represents a woman's ability to give flight to her thoughts and move at a moment's notice. When caught in a whirlwind of emotions, women can be wild as a wind and still maintain a calm serenity.

We associate elemental air with our very breath, the same way a mother is the breath of the human race. A lack of air will end the world; such is the glory of air and women on this Earth!

Like air, a woman is the symbol of new beginnings, youth, evolution, growth, and creativity. As such, it is associated with spring, the waxing moon, and sunrise. In the presence of women, things grow warmer and brighter, like the way the presence of air encourages life to grow.

Vulcan (Fire)

Fire is hot and intense, so like women, who hold the glow of passion and the power of transformation.

Fire can also be healing and transformative from the inside out. Women, like fire, can rage and burn everything and yet have the same inner strength to create a life!

Fire is the element of gleam, warmth and life. Its light drives back the dark and emanates warmth. Similarly, women are known for being innately skilled at giving life and warmth to emotions. Like fire, life is not possible without women.

Earth

Earth symbolizes stability and strength. Symbolically, a woman brings stability to her family and helps to solidify relationships with her constant efforts. Just as Earth imparts life, so does a woman nurture her family.

Earth produces and holds its gems and elements in her womb, so do women! Only a woman's womb can produce the "gems" of humanity. Like the earth, women can be both tough and soft, sometimes beautiful whereas sometimes minacious.

Space

Space is an elusive and expansive element. Though symbolically it is empty and has zero resistance, it is the source of substantial elements. It is a perfect allegory for a woman who is the source of life and who engulfs her world within its existence. She grows with every change around her, be it an emotional change or physical.

The Free Press Journal cites the five elements. "If there is no space, nothing can exist." Women resemble and reflect this quality; no human can exist on this Earth without a woman. Women need to be reminded that they embody miraculous potency, which should be utilized.

God created both Mother Nature and moms, gifting them equal strength and lovely qualities. It is said that mothers are the best creations of God, but moms in the twenty-first century are Herculean! They juggle their professions, motherhood, finances, shopping, relationships, and all while turning their houses into homes. Working mommies are breaking down the myths of women being useless and trifling, and are proving what the true essence of being a woman is!

The world is saluting the women who are exhibiting the strength that Mother Nature has gifted them.

As you read, I will give you some useful tips as well as explain exactly how each working mom embodies all five elements of the universe, and I'll introduce you to your inner strengths, capabilities, and superpowers!

> *"With so much inside her,*
> *A lot still has to come out to make her stand apart."*

Surf The Waves

Chapter 1

The Water

You Are Water – Sustaining and Potent

"I am Water. Soft enough to offer life. Tough enough to drown it away."

Rupi Kaur

Woman and water are the two most appealing, harmonious, and generative creations of God. Both are famous for beauty, craving and life. Like water, women flourish life and plant happiness in the family.

Being a woman, you also need to do what water does—find out a way through all the obstacles facing you and reach your true identity. You do so by making relevant adjustments and being fluid in your thoughts and actions. As a working mom, it is vital to tweak your methods to get the most out of your efforts.

And just like water, God has blessed women with productive qualities, so much so we are compared to Mother Nature. As a working mom, you can create better circumstances for your family and your career... but you need to master the tips.

Here are some practical productivity tips that will allow you to make the most of a twenty-four-hour day.

1. Identify Your Goal:

When an objective is in sight, things will become simpler. Focus on your goal, eliminate frivolous things, then watch that spring in your step and twinkle in your eye come to life.

2. Focus and Attention:

Multitasking is a strict no-no. Stay in the present in order to do justice to your tasks. Don't answer your work emails while playing with your child, nor chide your child while on the phone in a business meeting.

3. Be Human:

Though you need to be a superhuman to handle home, children and career, still try to be human. That may reduce your work-load. Hire people to do menial jobs for you and save your precious time.

4. Cut the Crap:

Do not ponder over frivolous things. Pay attention to your essential goals. Instead of fretting over your lush front lawn, see that your kids have watered the plants. Don't agitate if your housemaid has cooked lots of soup. See that you have a good amount of prepared meal that will be kept stored in your fridge.

5. Let Go:

Don't aspire to be a perfectionist! Be comfortable and let go of the minute details. See the larger picture and stay happy and natural.

6. Recharge:

Rejuvenation is vital. Don't assume it as a waste of time. Handling home, work, and family can really sap your energy. Recharging your batteries will allow you to relax.

7. Start with a Tough Task:

Usually we tend to push the difficult tasks off and prefer doing simpler things first. Do it the other way around. Finish the difficult task first and then move on to the easier task. Psychologically you will feel more productive, and a sense of accomplishment will prevail.

8. Stopwatch:

One effective way to speed up your work pace is to beat the clock. Set the timer or work with a stopwatch running. But don't let this make you nervous! Enjoy your race against the time.

9. Zero Distractions:

When you have a dedicated schedule to follow, do not allow any distractions to hinder you. Give your complete attention and commit to your tasks.

10. Health is Wealth:

Put your health on the highest pedestal, and it will skyrocket your productivity. A healthy mind and a healthy body will help you scale greater heights. Eating well and thinking positive will help you stay positive. Life will be a blessing for you.

11. Assign and Allocate:

Your kids can be your greatest asset. Try exploring their potential, and you will find that they love helping you. They can be of great help: watering plants, grocery shopping (make sure to give them a list or else your shopping budget will go overboard!), baking cookies, bill paying, filing your documents, etc. This will serve a dual purpose... while doing your mundane work, they will learn basic skills.

12. Smart Cooking:

How about some meal planning to save you time? Chopping vegetables and salads can be done for a few days in advance. Gravies and condiments can also be prepared ahead of time. You can make broths, soups, and freeze them. Loaves of bread and other accompaniments can also be done in advance.

It's all in your mind how to beat the odds. Keep your chin up and head held high! Believe in yourself, and watch your objectives get accomplished.

Be flexible... Be Natural.

Chapter 2

The Air

You Are Air – Light and Active

You may shoot me with your words,
You may cut me with your eyes,
You may kill me with your hatefulness,
But still, like air, I'll rise.

Maya Angelou

The importance of the presence of women can be understood by comparing women with air! Like air, a woman is also cool, light, subtle, flowing, sharp, and clear. Although air is invisible … but its effects are observable. Women's presence is also striking and soothing. Isn't it? We know what the women mean to the world!

As of now, we are specifically talking about working mothers. Please understand, you are a priority. Until you take care of yourself, nothing I suggest will work. Your self-care will start the moment you decide to embark.

Here are some rejuvenating chunks of advice that will go a long way to you taking care of yourself, and make you light and active like the air.

13. Don't Maintain a Strict Regimen:

Care about your choices, needs, and desires. Carve out free time from your routine, so it doesn't become stale. By gifting yourself some "me time" it will increase your core happiness. Behave non-rigidly with yourself and don't behave like a regimen.

14. Help Yourself Like You do Others:

You deserve to be cared for like your child and other family members. Take care of yourself by doing your favorite things such as listening to music, having a session at a spa or aroma bath, working out or taking guitar classes. This will help you feel like a breeze—light and refreshing. Reading self-help or motivational books can help solve inner turmoil you may be facing.

15. Install a Fitness App:

Fitness or self-card apps can be great to connect with other people and can also remind and motivate you to take care of your needs.

16. Safeguard Yourself:

Sometimes we come in contact with people or situations that drain our brain, and we find ourselves unable extract ourselves from that toxic situation. To be light like air and be the best working mommy, you need to learn how to safeguard yourself from such circumstances. They can be as innocuous as a negative neighbor, an annoying relative, or maybe a critical friend. Keeping them at bay will help remove you from negative energy.

17. Get a Nice Massage:

Get a gentle massage at least every two weeks. These days we have different types of massages such as: stone massage, aromatherapy massage, or trigger point massage. Massages have a tremendous therapeutic effect, and can help you feel refreshed.

18. Regularly Try Beauty Sessions:

A woman - no matter a working woman or a housewife, who are also working—love to look beautiful. If feeling beautiful makes you happy, why not try it? You can go for a facial, a nice haircut, pedicure, or manicure. You don't need to spend all day but just a little time alone to feel pampered. Or just get your nails done in Nail-Art Centers! Your beauty sessions can get wrapped up within a reasonable time.

19. Mornings are Mesmerizing:

The world is beautiful and especially the mornings. Having quiet time with your partner, just sipping a cup of tea or coffee while looking out over the rising sun can be blissful, as it comes with minimal distractions. Mornings can become stress busters for you and the time spent in this way can be cherishable. If you prefer your alone time, you can listen to your favorite music, meditate, take a walk or even use the time to go to the gym. Mornings are a fresh start; learn to make the most of them.

20. Don't Forget Your Roots:

Stay close and connected to your family; they are your roots. Family love is a magic potion that can keep you emotionally healthy. Not properly tending the "roots" can cause the flowers and leaves in your life to wither. Family time can make you feel supported and refreshed.

21. Use Acupressure to Kill Body Ache or Stress:

If you are not physically healthy, make sure to sort it out, because if your health is at risk, it can disturb your focus, dedication, and passion toward your family and your job. Acupressure is an ancient and reliable therapy that can provide you with effective relief.

22. Look after Your Mental Health:

After taking care of your physical health, you should also look after your mental care. While playing the dual role of career woman and mommy, and trying to perform both to the fullest, you may feel tired and drained.

Light meditational music, or just watching TV shows can help. Keeping connections with family and friends, help you relieve stress.

23. Take Advantage of Social Media:

As a human being, it is imperative to connect with one another. Connections bring a soothing assurance and comfort to your mind. When you hear how other women are going through the same emotions you are, it is comforting to know you are not alone. Networking leads to sharing and empathizing that can lead to innovative solutions. Being a working mommy isn't a static process. It is ever-evolving and dynamic and can be bettered with creative explorations.

We are not suggesting trolling on a variety of social media platforms; this it is about networking. Facebook, Twitter, LinkedIn, etc. can be useful. Fruitful interactions will demand some time and effort before successful networking will gather traction.

24. Look Around for Other Working Mommies:

You can connect to your tribe within your family circle, your child's school, your friends and colleagues, as well as sports centers and recreational facilities. Scan through relevant parenting forums as well!

25. Interact and Enjoy:

To feel lighter and happier, it is pivotal to interact with like-minded people. Start a group or plan a lunch date with your tribe members. Talk to them and, more importantly, listen to them. They are your real life encyclopedias! Many creative solutions and innovative hacks can be learned and taught mutually.

Be receptive to people and situations around you, and soon you will connect with working moms like you.

26. Work as a Volunteer:

Find some time during lean work days and be a volunteer at your kid's school. Talk to the teacher and offer to help at an upcoming function or fundraising event. You may have to stretch your schedule a little bit, but then this will be useful for you and your child's social esteem.

That kind of involvement can be like a balm to your guilt-ridden mind, and a new sense of calm befall you, and your child will feel loved and attended by you—not to mention proud of your volunteering!

27. Manage Your the Time:

The working mommy needs to manage her time to achieve the most from her day. Time management isn't rocket science, and you can excel with simple yet effective tips. Carving a ten-minute breather out of your hectic schedule will make you feel empowered. Even slightly tweaking your choreographed life will take your time management to the next level.

By managing your time and utilizing it effectively, you can make yourself and others happy, and your life will be even more satisfactory.

28. Get Ample Sleep:

While maintaining these many roles, you need to take care of yourself not only by eating healthy food, keeping physically fit, and taking care of your mental health but also by making sure to have sound and ample sleep!

Don't neglect your daily sleep needs. Even if you have tons of work and responsibilities, you should keep in mind that less sleep can affect your performance the next day. By taking fewer measures of sleep, you will put your health in danger. Try napping when possible to allow your mind and body rest; this can make you light and fresh.

29. Divide your Life and Time:

To play both the roles peacefully and perfectly, you need to divide your days into two parts. Schedule your day, and cover both your duties. Reserve your hours for home and work separately, and don't allow intermingling. It will stress you to attempt both responsibilities simultaneously.

Even when you are free during office hours, don't shift your attention to home and family. And when you are with your kids, be their mommy *only*; don't work while playing or talking with them.

30. Avoid Unnecessary Burdens:

Filter your tasks according to priorities and importance. Don't invest your capabilities and time on unnecessary things. Check your schedule and decide to eliminate unnecessary items or tasks.

Stay empowered and decline less important meetings. By avoiding unnecessary plans, you can free yourself and feel light like air.

31. Stay Away from the Things that Kill Time:

Stay away from useless things like net-surfing, video games, and chatting with the neighbors. We do so many useless things to satisfy someone else, or we follow trends that eat away the hours! What can start as a two-minute break can turn into precious hours.

32. Teach Your Family:

As a working woman, you need to take care of yourself, and as you take care of your family members, they should in turn help take care of you.

Do not feel ashamed by accepting the help. It's not a big deal if your husband fixes his evening snack. Let them help if they can! Allow your children to clean up their messy rooms. You don't always need to be physically present. You should delegate work to maximize your potential.

33. Utilize Your Lunch Breaks for Maximum Fun:

A lot can be done during small pockets of time, like your lunch break. Give yourself a break during that window of time. For example, you can give yourself a manicure, catch a quick nap, make online purchases, read your favorite book or magazine, or even listen to music that can rejuvenate you.

34. Make a Habit of Writing Lists:

Start making a pen and paper list for all the tasks to be done. It's an easy way to record pending tasks, and as you complete each tasks, strike off the entry. This can have a psychological effect and make you feel accomplished.

It also helps in keeping the mind clear of cluttering thoughts.

35. Automate your Life:

Learn the benefit of automation. You can feel light by enabling auto-payment for your bills, or auto-delivery of groceries or medicines. This can conserve your time and energy.

36. Save your Time by Promptly Working:

Prompt action can go a long way in saving time. Don't put off your tasks; do them beforehand. For example, you can rinse your dishes just as you finish your meal, or fold and stack clothes right after changing; pack the bag in the morning for your evening gym workout, or prepare meals for the following day. These practices will save a lot of time, and you will remain stress free if you finish such preparations beforehand.

37. Give Yourself a Treat Sometimes:

If you are a working woman and a mommy also, it doesn't mean you should always be anxious and frustrated! If you are not finding your life perfect, you need to make some changes in your thinking as well as in your routine.

You deserve to be happy every day. If you dedicate four days per week taking care of your job and family, you should also devote at least two days in pampering yourself. If you are feeling frustrated with the life you are living, you are trying to fit too much in your hours; don't do that.

Start pampering yourself. You can ordering a cake or ice cream instead of baking or preparing yourself. Or maybe arrange an outing to a water park or movie with your family. You can also arrange a date with your hubby, which can refresh your relationship. So, just learn to say 'No' - even to yourself.

38. Stock and Store:

It is beneficial to stock and store essential things in your home. It will help to prevent last-minute sprinting to the market. Stock up on your kids favorite ready-to-eat snacks, or medicines and groceries. Such things should always be in your pantry.

Refresh Yourself – Be a Perfect Mommy

Chapter 3

The Vulcan

You Are Vulcan [Fire] – Passionate & Glowing

"Man may have discovered fire, but women discovered how to play with it."

Candace Bushnell

Fire is the driving force behind all life process, and so are women. When in a balanced state, fire induces power, confidence and flame. Women also induce power and energy in all family members and they nurture life within the family. Women have the ability to strengthen the bonds of love and care among family members.

You are the flame for the family who enlightens their paths and energizes their beings. Keep in mind that you, too, need the power to enhance your inner soul.

Below are some more fiery tips for you.

39. It is All in Your Mind:

Your mind is a powerhouse. All the miracles that you have been dreaming of are brewing up in your mind. Hone and harness your passionate fire and work accordingly.

Develop a fire-like mind, and you may win all odds.

40. Accept the Tribulations:

Life will undoubtedly throw lemons at you. Catch them, squeeze them to make lemonade, and take a refreshing sip! Acceptance of tough situations will come only with a strong and sharp mind. Find smart solutions and materialize them.

The things or situations that are seemingly troublesome to you today might change into a blessing tomorrow. Just have patience and courage… and search for that magical element. Your curse may evolve into a blessing.

If you are dedicated, you will see a silver lining behind the clouds, and it will help you to make lemonade out of lemons.

41. You are Not a Victim:

Stop being a martyr. Identify your emotional and material needs and replace them with a confident mind. It is fine to address your own requirements. Don't be apologetic for fulfilling your dreams. After all, you were not born a victim! Instead, give your goals and desires equal importance, just like you do for family members. Your dreams are important, and your family should help you in fulfilling them. That is what a family is meant to be!

42. Say it Out Loud:

It is essential to think intelligently and to speak your mind. Be vocal with a firm and a polite tone. Nothing is wrong in expressing what you feel about a particular action or situation.

43. Making your Mind Stronger

Problems will keep on erupting. Sometimes your kids will draw your energy, and other times, your profession will tear your hair out. Illuminate your mind to develop an emotional glow to face any situation. Read good books that can guide you in handling tough situations. Good self-improvement books and classic literature like Dale Carnegie, Stephen R. Covey, Robin Sharma, and Napoleon Hill can guide you well. Make your mind sharper by reading from these great minds.

44. Manage Anxiety and Fears:

Once fears and anxiety are confronted, you become mentally stronger. It might be slightly uncomfortable, but train your mind to flight mode instead of fleeing mode. Leap beyond your uneasiness and manage your fears and make your mind more energetic.

45. Get help from Meditation:

To illuminate your mind and set your fire on, you should consider meditation. This Indian tool has been proven to work since ancient times. A few minutes dedicated to serene mediation with meditation music can not only strengthen your mind but can also heal you physically and emotionally. Meditation can give you strength to bless you with new life.

46. Give Importance to Your Health:

Your optimum health and all the aspects of wellness are of vital importance for your career as well as motherhood. Be sure to take care of *all* aspects of health and wellness, and begin at a young age. Once you reach thirty, your body stops making new cells, and after forty years of age, your body becomes vulnerable to all sorts of disease, especially those with lifestyle choices. If you practice exercise, yoga asanas, and meditation from a young age, you will limit your exposure to disease. So, give importance to your health.

47. Practice Positive Thinking:

Being an educated woman and reading this book, I am sure you must have ome across the books, articles, or eBooks on positive thinking. But still, sometimes we feel so dejected and cheated that we start harnessing negativity inside our souls. That can disturb our beings. It is better to toss this negativity out of your brain and be positive, which will make you feel good. It can rejuvenate you.

48. Prioritize:

When you prioritize things in your mind, you strengthen your cerebral matter. Create visual clues to remember essential things. This will create order inside your mind and can help you tackle projects according to their importance. All the fluff and useless information will also get sifted away. Allocate one project at a time. This will keep you strongly motivated.

49. Be Grateful:

The emotion of gratitude holds immense potential to steer you out of feelings of anxiety. Count your blessings, and your fears will take a backseat. Being grateful will strengthen your mind to take up newer challenges. Being thankful in life is something that can make you happy from the inside. Living this way, you can be more productive and creative.

50. Identify Good or Bad Emotions:

It is true that a mommy needs to be emotional. But it is crucial to tag the positive (happy) and negative (sad) emotions in order to handle the waves of emotions properly. If you learn this art of managing emotions, it will help you control them instead of them controlling you.

Being a mommy, you need to understand your feelings for your child. You should rectify the feelings that arise because of negative issues related to your child like anxiety, fear or annoyance. Learn to control them and save your emotional health. Identify the triggers of negative emotions and avoid them; it will help you to be a better mom.

51. Harness that Fire Inside You:

No one can deny that an intangible caliber needed by every working mommy is an invariable amount of sheer motivation. Illuminating the fire will bring forth that ceaseless passion to conquer your objectives. Your motivation must stay glowing and bright to keep you raring to go, day after day and year after year.

52. Learn to be Happy from the Inside:

You, your profession, and your child will be considered blessed and will flourish if you learn how to be happy from inside. Your happiness will be seen in your work, and your satisfaction will appear in the happiness of your child. If you want to raise a happy child while maintaining a dynamic career, you need to learn the art of being satisfied from within. You can take the help of books on positivity or happiness in life.

53. This too shall Pass:

Keep chanting this mantra to feel good. Your struggle will get transformed into joys once your children grow up and become your support. Don't fret while changing diapers; very soon, your brood is going to be your pride - imagine yourselves strutting stylishly in a shopping mall. Yawning at your desktop will not be forever. This too shall pass

54. Have Patience:

Stay patient. Things may not work the way you want every time. Wait for the tide to turn. Rushing will only muddle things up. Sit back and look around; things are better than before and will be even better in the future.

55. Don't Overthink:

Too much thinking leads to inactivity and saps your motivation. Analysis works to a point, and after that it becomes a mental paralysis. Be quick to kindle your fire to shine brightly.

56. Be Present in the Present:

Stay in the present to remain calm and patient. Congregate your attention on one thing and complete it successfully. When with your kids, give them 100 percent of your time and attention. Leave all your office worries behind and bask in the sunshine of your kids' smiles. Half-done tasks will stay in your mind and diminish your enthusiasm.

57. Learn to Say No:

Decline what you can't do or don't want to do. Graciously decline the invitations you cannot attend; say no to work favors and your associates' requests. You are allowed to say no to whatever you deem appropriate. Chip in for worthwhile activities, and politely decline everything else. This will help you take control of your life.

58. Evoke Your Identity:

With so much going within your universe, keep your sanity intact. You are a hub of your world, and you must nurture yourself, and maintain a unique identity. Find time to attend the jam show from your favorite band. Have a lavish lunch in the company of your true self.

Stay Upbeat...Be a Mommy.

Chapter 4

The Earth

You Are Earth - Stable and Grounded

*"The Women of Our World are like Mother Earth.
They don't just give life to the next generation
but also the Hope."*

Avijeet Das

Remember, women are meant for life and hope, the same as Mother Earth. Your stability and strength can rejuvenate your family's lives. Just a smile on your face can provide thousands of meanings of happiness.

If you are a mother and are worried about your role as a working mommy, just remind yourself that you are as mighty as Mother Earth! You have endless power in your soul, and there is every reason you will be successful in your two roles and equally beautifully at the same time - if you are willing.

What do you need to do? You must be stable in mind and grounded in perspective, like the Earth, and you must get rid of the feeling of being a victim. You are a supermom, and it is natural to stay busy and engaged all the time. Look beyond your horizon. A whole Working Mom's Tribe is waiting to greet you with their tired yet cheerful smiles.

Compare yourself to Earth. Let's strengthen and fortify your inner soul and juggle both the roles with equal amounts of zeal, potency, and warmth.

Here are some vital strengthening (Earthly) tips:

59. Balancing Work and Home:

I know balancing your profession and home calls for a lot of focus, hard work and dedication. But remember the Earth revolves without getting tired or frustrated, and that she is able to do because of the rain, chilled breezes, and warm zephyrs. In the same manner, if you add entertainment and do the things you love, you will be able to balance your profession and home with equal zeal each day.

While balancing your work and home, you need not be too utopian in your expectations. You are not a robot! Make a plan that will make you happy and stay focused on that plan - the rest will follow.

60. The Care of Your Child:

Your priority is your child. You can halt your job or profession for at least one year. Your baby's first year is vital. It is necessary to be with her at least for an year.

You can work from home during this period, and after the year, you may attempt a part-time job. The baby needs a mommy in the initial years, and after that, you can look for a responsible and reliable babysitter or nanny. Hire those who are experienced and recommended by families. Having your child handed over to a reliable nanny will take away a major chunk of your worry.

61. Keep Mornings Clutter Free:

A chaotic morning should be the last way to start. Plan ahead and do chores beforehand to keep your mornings smooth and serene. Lay out your children's and your clothes, fill the water bottles, pack the fruit boxes, decide the breakfast menu, and check the bags and purses, etc. in advance. These small tasks seem mundane but take up chunks of time.

62. Scheduling the Whole Week on Sunday:

Keep a calendar handy to jot down significant chores, events, and dates. Schedule the essential things to avoid missing anything. This kind of scheduling can be done on Sunday and will help set your mind free during the week. This will keep you organized and save a lot of your time and money.

63. Share with Other Working Mommies:

Meeting other working moms will help you feel good, knowing they feel exactly like you. Giggle over how no one noticed your new hairstyle and how your delicious cooking is taken for granted, even after your long day at work.

64. Say No to Multitasking:

I would recommend to not multitask while spending time with your kids. Instead, give them your undivided attention. It is easy to get distracted by work while being at home and vice-versa.

Working mommies need to learn how to minimize distractions. Set time limits for checking your email at home. Also, you can watch less TV to spend quality time with your spouse. After all, multitasking is not always beneficial. Your kids need you, just like saplings need water - ample and undivided! So always give them your love and attention when they need it badly.

65. Intake of Vitamin 'I':

A perfect balance between your home and work can be maintained by nourishing yourself with vitamin 'I.' Take a nap, or a swim, or maybe read your favorite book to refresh yourself. Recharge your physical and mental batteries to keep you going.

66. No Self-Shaming, please:

You are a working mommy and a responsible life partner. But before that, you are a human being, so it is perfectly natural to want a sweet gesture of thankfulness from your spouse or those magical words, thank you, which express recognition of your efforts. And really, you deserve it! Do not feel shame if your unconscious mind knocks it to your heart. You can demand thanks from your family.

67. Self-Appreciation:

Appreciate your efforts and feel all the love you give to your family. Tell yourself how incredible you are! Acknowledge your importance. This can rejuvenate your days, and will fill you with fresh energy to perform those hectic duties again the next day.

68. Ask for Short Leaves:

Be open and upfront with your employer. Don't be apologetic while asking for an abrupt short leave. It is not a crime to look after your family and your responsibilities. Be confident and demand it. Developing a healthy relationship with your employer will be helpful at such times.

69. Ask for Help:

Sometimes office works really sucks! There are moments when you face problems balancing unavoidable duties with your kids or family, as well as your responsibilities toward work! In such situations, go ahead and ask for favors from your colleagues. It's perfectly okay. Taking help will keep you on track, and you can, of course, repay back when they are in need.

70. Stay Relaxed if You get off Track:

If your schedule is going haywire, don't fret. It is perfectly normal to have your planning go a little off track. Give yourself a breather instead of a self-lashing.

Striking a balance between home and work shouldn't be a punishment. Be spontaneous and enjoy the situation. Treat home and work as two different worlds that need juggling for you to find your happiness.

Be Striking... Be A Wonderful Mommy!

Chapter 5

The Space

You Are Space - Vast and Expansive

"Women hold up more than half the sky. They represent much of the world's unrealized potential."

Ban Ki-moon

Space is refreshing, light, and subtle. Women are also light and delicate. Women also have no limits and work hard without any form or boundaries. Like space, women are also able to take different shapes. Similarly, women introduce knowledge and awareness in children to help them understand new and creative ideas.

When women do so much for the family, they require some tips to rejuvenate their energies every night, so that they can work the next morning with equal zeal and happiness.

So, dear woman, to unveil that unrealized potential inside you, read these vitalizing nuggets of wisdom, apply them, and share with many. Here are a few more points to cherish in your everyday life:

71. Focus on Your Goals:

To intelligently achieve success in your profession and as a mommy, it is vital to keep your goals clear and focused. Whether it's about your child's life or your own, brainstorm thoroughly about your goals, and once you decide be focused!

If you wish to avoid being confused or disturbed, the best way is to think things through before deciding the goals.

No matter what the decision, you should be clear and confident so that you know where you are heading.

72. Plan Your Day and Rule It:

To achieve success in the roles of a mommy as well as a working woman, you need to plan your day and life perfectly and diligently. You are the master of your life and time, just make proper use of it.

You can rule your life yourself. Take suggestions from others - family or friends - but make the final decision as your personal choice. This way, you won't regret it in the future. Planning and following the plan both are important. After all, it's your life, and you have the right to choose how you want to live it.

73. Take Help from Outsourcing:

Today we are living in an era where we have to arrange a lot of functions. Many things we plan today, our mothers did not have to plan twenty-five years ago.

But if you make grand arrangements, always remember that you can outsource such preparations. Sometimes you can even outsource your office work. If there is something you cannot do or don't want to do, you can outsource it. Help yourself to make your life comfortable and pleasant.

74. Avoid Driving:

Today we are doing everything ourselves! We are helping our kids in studies, buying groceries, handling medical needs of the family, cooking and providing lunch boxes, finishing office files, and whatnot!

Here is a suggestion to avoid driving, if possible. Women - especially working women - are living a stressful life, so by skipping driving, you can get a peaceful ride in your vehicle or by utilizing public transport. You can listen to your favorite music, take a nap, or just chat with fellow passengers while traveling. Driving is stressful, so instead of driving, you can relax at this time.

Chapter 6

Quick Tips

75. Keep time for your physical, mental, and emotional unwinding.
76. If traveling by public transport, take a ten-minute power nap.
77. Breathe deeply. It has a substantial calming effects.
78. Always keep something handy to eat in your handbag. Your hectic schedule may make you irritable due to small bouts of hunger.
79. Remember to enjoy the journey called LIFE. If certain things aren't working the way you want, leave them as they are.
80. People will advise you or give their expert opinion. Ignore them. Do it the way it suits you and your family.
81. Free yourself of emotional baggage. Steer away from negative and toxic people.
82. Disable your social media notifications.
83. Stop catering to others' expectations.
84. Accept your limitations and stop running after "elusive perfection."

85. At times it is advisable to become deaf, dumb and blind... especially around negative people.

86. Learn to be conveniently forgetful when useless events are happening.

87. Inculcate independence in your children. You will be proud of them in later years.

88. Pray daily, and be full of gratitude toward the universe.

Chapter 7

The Spouse Help

After discussing all the points of time management, taking care of your physical and mental health, and growing your connectivity, we will now talk about the help your spouse can provide. Your spouse is your arsenal, indeed. Before we tell you how to clue-in your spouse for support, here is one small write-up you may want to ask your spouse to read.

Dear Hubby,

With all the eternal love I hold for you in my heart, I want to say that I am so very tired. Every time you exasperate at me, I want to yell, throw a big fit, and simply travel to the moon just to take a relaxing nap.

I am always carrying mountain-sized guilt that I am failing every day as a wife, as a mother, and as a worker! Serving you the same dish for three meals in a row is the last thing I want to do but.

Now, don't say that I chose to be a working mom! I know it's my choice. But with our baby keeping me awake all night, I get a sense of relief at work. But after an hour I start thinking about our little angel.

I would love to be a stay-at-home mom, but I equally love my work. I feel useful! I want my kids to learn the importance of being a hard worker. Despite this, my guilt continues.

Honey, I need your help! Do you understand and can you see how hard I am struggling? Whenever I am cranky, be patient. Perhaps I've had a bad day at work, and the baby isn't behaving. Whenever you see me dozing off on the couch, let me lay there. That's my way of rejuvenating my physical and mental batteries. When I decline our date night, please, understand that would sometimes prefer nestling in bed and have a frozen dinner instead of an elaborate meal in a fancy restaurant.

And when I want to go out with friends, don't think I am selfish. My friends energize me. Help me feel better about socializing, so that I don't lose my inner self.

All those times, when you took care of our kids while I was out, I appreciated it. Did I say that? The way you fed them, nurse them, teach them, and play with them, makes me feel relaxed. I know it gets very demanding, but thanks for being there.

I am sure both of us will get past this hectic time in our lives. Soon this strife will be past us, and our beautiful family will be even more beautiful and happier.

-Your working wife!

Once you make your husband read this letter, it will be easier for you to pull him in to aid you. Get rid of the age-old conditioning that only you are responsible for your family.

89. Ask Your Spouse to Help You:

The help of your spouse will undoubtedly lead to the lightening of your mental and physical burden. When you know he is there with you, you will feel energized, helping you focus more consistently.

90. Make Him Feel Important:

You know how men are! They want you to make them feel important. It is going to be a win-win situation for both of you, if you train him to do menial stuff that when unattended can build up considerably. He can make you a coffee, warm up the soup, stack the dishwasher, pay the bills, and much more. He is an integral part of your life and thus deserves to be treated importantly.

91. Show Your Reliance:

"Relying upon" is an important emotion signifying trust. By showing him you rely on him, it will engage him. Don't fret by the way he messed up cooking last time. It's okay if he isn't folding the laundry the way you do. Stay cool and calm. He may not know the nuances of the household, but his efforts to unburden you should be appreciated.

92. Utilize His Talent:

Use the talent of your spouse to your benefit. He could be good at cooking, teaching kids, car maintenance, shopping... whatever. Make optimal use of his skills. Let him be the master of his expertise and sit back to see how he alleviates your worries.

93. Always Appreciate His Role:

This is coming full circle. As we discussed at the beginning of this eBook, appreciation is solicited by everyone. Appreciate your spouse for whatever he does for the family and watch his smile grow.

94. Understand His Nature:

Your life partner is your world to you and vice versa. Nature has uniquely created each individual. It is imperative you both accept each other for who you are, and you should never try to change his fundamental nature. If you understand this and accept him, he will support you the way you are.

95. Help Him in His ventures:

We should keep in mind the way in which we need our partner's support and help is equal to the way they need ours. Marital relations are also a give-and-take. You should always be available when your hubby needs your support and time, and vice versa. Your mutual understanding will create a robust support system for both of you.

96. Let Him Know the Ongoing Things in Your Life:

You should involve your partner in your career, whether a job, business, or profession. If he know all the ins-and-outs of your work day, he will be interested and will understand the need for getting involved.

Your spouse is your inherent strength. If he is with you, half the battle is won. You should harness his support to sail ahead!

Spouse, Spouse! Come to My Aid.

Chapter 8

The Five Unique Qualities

We have come to a point where you are equipped with weapons and suggestions to start a new life. You have become a mommy, and now you need to prove yourself the "Best Mommy." Utilize the advice given in this book by successful members of your tribe; it will change your world.

Below given are five prime punches - the qualities that are of prime importance. Without these five tips, your journey to your goal may become unnerving:

97. Water: Flexibility Counts.

Be as flexible as you can. It will help maintain relations and have compassion with other family members. It will be an asset to you.

98. Air: Speed is the Key.

As a working mommy you are trying to extract the maximum out of your twenty-four hours. And without acquiring speed, you can't do it. It is important to learn to finish jobs quickly. To prove yourself the best mommy, you need to become fast.

99. Vulcan (Fire): Your Courage can Change Your World.

Courage is a quality you need throughout your life. Being a woman, you will find yourself in unpleasant situations. It's only your courage that can drag you out from trouble. Learn to be courageous, and can seek brave friends, or you can read books about courage. Your struggle cannot convert into triumph until you are full of heroism.

100. Earth: Your Willpower is Your Triumph.

Willpower is something that can drive you. Without stubborn willpower, you cannot fulfill your dreams. Always understand the value of willpower, and it will encourage you in tough times.

101. Space: Perseverance can Prove You a Winner.

The one quality that is a must in your life is perseverance. Do not ever forget to pursue the track that can bring you close to your dreams. Fall, then rise again. But never forget your goal. To be successful and to create your identity, you need perseverance.

Always try to cultivate these qualities within yourself. They are a requisite.

I wish you Golden Luck for all your ventures. And I hope this guide will be a favorite of yours and help you to rise ahead in your journey.

How to Use This Guide

The WAVES

"You contain all the waves inside you. You just need to learn how to surf on them."

Nehal. VRK

If you have picked up this book, it means you are probably a working woman and are either expecting, or have already become a mom. So, congrats, and welcome to your new role, which will be filled with love, passion, confidence, and power.

How to Use this Guide?

It's simple!

Case 1:

If you are expecting a baby, read over and study the tips as you count down to your delivery date. And follow your plan. It will be beneficial to complete this book long before your due date. After the eighth month, days will become somewhat tough for you.

Case 2:

In case if you already have your baby, you may find little time to study this book as you hold those tiny fingers in your hand. However, you can set a target date to finish this book. Snatch a few moments to read every day—maybe while feeding the baby or while she is napping.

This book was deliberately written in bullet form to make the tips manageable and easier to digest and remember.

Set the target and follow your plan. Complete this book once, then mark the points you feel are written for you. And if needed, make your own list on the blank page given at the end of the book.

Creating your own list will be specific to you and be a reminder whenever you go off track.

I hope you to extract the most out of this book, which was written with you in mind. May these 101 tips prove helpful.

Upcoming Book

Czarina Book 2- 'From Screen to Sky' preaches and speaks the subject that every parent wishes to discuss. The screens have engulfed our children's lives, and we are worried. Isn't your soul sigh for swiping away the digital screens around your kid? Don't you want to hold your kid's hand and take him to the real beautiful world scattered on the planet? Don't you wish the kid should experience those tiny raindrops on his cheeks & inhale the smell of monsoon, all around? Worried? Read this book to understand how you can teach your child the difference between 'Real Experiences' & 'Digital World'.......Hold his hand and bring him to the Real-world......From Screen to Sky.

www.ingramcontent.com/pod-product-compliance
Lightning Source LLC
LaVergne TN
LVHW021304080526
838199LV00090B/6016